BEST MU

CW00327922

Everyone thinks that their Mum
Is the best Mum in the world.
They're wrong!
Mine is!

I'm giving my Mum big bear hugs
'Cause she's the best Mum
Anyone could wish for.

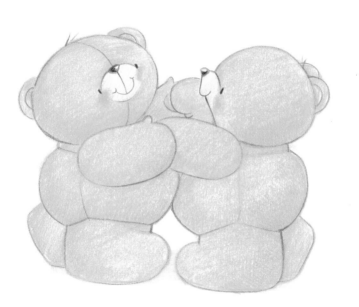

It only takes one flower to say,
'I love you, Mum.'

Whenever my world
Turns upside down,
My Mum's there
To make sense of everything.
Thanks, Mum.

I'll sing it in the bathtub
I'll bang it on my drum.
So that all the world will know,
How much I love my Mum.

I'm catching wonderful things
To give to my Mum,
Because she's such
A wonderful person.

I'm not the only person
Who thinks my Mum's special.
Everyone she meets thinks so too.

My Mum gave me roots
So I could bloom
Like these plants.
And she gave me wings
So that I could fly
Like these butterflies.
Thanks, Mum.

My Mum's like the sun
On a beautiful summer's day,
She makes me feel warm all over.

If anyone deserves a treat
It's my Mum.
Because she's the best there is.

My Mum is so loving and caring
That she really knocks me over.

I've climbed to the top of the pile
To tell my Mum
What a special person she is.

My Mum's funny.
My Mum's wise.
Kindness shines from
My Mum's eyes.

Tell your Mum you love her.
And you'll always be her friend
Tell your Mum you love her
And will do 'til time's end.

Wherever she goes,
My Mum fills the world
With friendship.

When my Mum smiles
The whole world lights up
With happiness...

Always remember that if
It wasn't for your Mum,
You wouldn't be here!

If it wasn't for you, Mum,
Life wouldn't be the same.

I'll give you this flower, Mum.
Thanks for what you do.
Then I'll kiss and cuddle you
Because you love me too.

If anyone deserves
All the good things in life,
It's you, Mum.
Thank you.

I don't have to give you flowers
To say that you're the
Best Mum in the world.
But I wanted to,
Because you are.

Mum, when I see you smile
I feel lighter
Than a cloud of butterflies.

Our Mum loves us all the same
When we're good or bad.
She makes us happy with a kiss
And hugs us when we're sad.

Mums are always there
To wipe away your tears
When things go wrong.
That's why they're such
Extra-special people.

If anyone deserves
To have the boat pushed out,
It's you, Mum, - you're the best.

My Mum's more than just a Mum.
She's my best friend too.

I want to paint 'I LOVE YOU MUM'
In letters ten feet high.
I want to paint 'THANK YOU MUM'
Right across the sky.

My Mum deserves the
Biggest flower there is.
Because she's the
Best Mum there is.

A bouquet of love
For the most special
Person in the world.
You, Mum.

There's just one more thing
I want to say, Mum.
Thank you.
And I love you.
Okay, I know that's two things -
But who's counting?

It's time to put your feet up,
Best Mum in the World.